SOCRATES

The Public Conscience of Golden Age Athens

THE LIBRARY OF GREEK PHILOSOPHERS™

SOCRATES

The Public Conscience of Golden Age Athens

Jun Lim

The Rosen Publishing Group, Inc., New York

To my sister, Toy, who taught me to question, and to my brother, Gee, who always had questions.

Published in 2006 by The Rosen Publishing Group, Inc.
29 East 21st Street, New York, NY 10010

Library of Congress Cataloging-in-Publication Data

Lim, Jun.
Socrates: the public conscience of Golden Age Athens/
Jun Lim.—1st ed.
    p. cm.—(The library of Greek philosophers)
Includes bibliographical references (p.) and index.
ISBN 1-4042-0564-0 (library binding)
1. Socrates.
I. Title. II. Series.
B316.L65 2007
183'.2—dc22
                                                    2005012259

Printed in China

On the cover: Background: Jacques-Louis David's 1787 oil painting *The Death of Socrates.* Inset: A Greek marble bust of Socrates from circa the fourth century BC.

CONTENTS

INTRODUCTION

During the fifth century BC, Athens was one of the most powerful city-states in the Mediterranean. Its military was so strong that its outlying neighbors turned to its troops for protection. The city was the scene of many glorious military, artistic, and political triumphs, including the development of the world's first democratic system. Athenians were happy with their government and felt safe from most dangers. From this position of strength and security, Athenian society gave rise to institutions and ways of thinking that are still influential to many nations of the world today.

This great era of Athenian history is known as its golden age, and some of its chief achievements were in the area

Beginning in the early sixth century BC, the agora of Athens was the city-state's public gathering place, a sort of town square or marketplace. In it, political, commercial, religious, cultural, and educational activities took place. Important buildings and monuments around the agora included temples, altars, council assemblies, various stores, an auditorium and gymnasium, and monuments to legendary figures and war heroes. A twentieth-century watercolor by Peter Connolly of the agora circa 400 BC appears above.

of philosophy. Heated discussions about science, truth, and morality would erupt in Athens's crowded marketplaces, captivating, enlightening, and informally educating those who stopped to listen. Learning was no longer a luxury reserved for only the educated and leisure classes. The streets of Athens served as a breeding ground for the philosophical ideas that we still study and practice in modern times. This philosophical theater had its regular scholars who visited daily the city's public gathering places, refining their skills of argument. Ordinary untrained bystanders would also jump into these passionate

Socrates' influence spread far beyond his own time, place, and culture, and his reputation only increased with the passing years. The image at left is from a sixteenth-century fresco, or wall painting, in the Augustinian monastery of Atotonilco el Grande in Hidalgo, Mexico. The image is part of a series in which St. Augustine appears alongside the great philosophers of antiquity, who, though pagan, were thought to have anticipated the moral and ethical teachings of Jesus.

discussions. Standing prominently in the limelight of this philosophical stage was a man named Socrates.

Socrates was an active participant in this intellectual give and take. He challenged anyone walking through Athens's marketplace to a contest of verbal and mental skill, regardless of the person's age or status. He heckled passersby until they would agree to give him their definitions of morality, truth, and virtue. He devoted decades of his life to these debates, inspiring people to question their assumptions and examine their own moral characters. He had a large following of young, curious intellectuals

who would engage in debates with him and seek the wisdom he seemed to possess.

Socrates' core interest in morality and ethics—knowing what is right and acting accordingly—did not change over his lifetime, but Athens did. At the turn of the fourth century BC, Athens saw its democracy suspended, many of its citizens killed by disease and war, and its sense of security destroyed. As much as Socrates was a product of the stimulating era, he ultimately became its victim. When Athens fell from its golden age perch, the once progressive society that fostered Socrates' outspoken views turned on him and condemned and executed the much-respected leader for his challenging ideas.

Once confronted with war, defeat, disease, and death, one of the most progressive societies in history suddenly became capable of turning a seventy-one-year-old philosopher into a scapegoat who was forced to bear the burden of Athens's recent setbacks and failings. Despite the fact that Socrates had dedicated the majority of his life urging people to lead virtuous, civic-minded lives, in the end, the very society he sought to nurture and improve permitted the execution of one of the greatest thinkers the world has ever known.

1 SOCRATES' YOUTH, EDUCATION, AND INFLUENCES

There is little that is known for certain about the details of Socrates' life. He never kept any written records on his life or his philosophies. This may indicate that he did not believe that he would become so influential a thinker. In addition, his most important quest was always for truth, not fame, wealth, followers, or a historical legacy.

Whatever Socrates' reasoning for not writing anything down, it has long frustrated historians and scholars who, centuries after his death, continue to rummage for clues about his life. Nothing of a biographical nature was written about him while he was still living. As a consequence, there is doubt even about the few "facts" that have survived through time concerning his personal life. The few definite details about Socrates' life that scholars have discovered are drawn from secondhand sources penned by just three men—Aristophanes, Plato, and Xenophon. Most of their works were written after Socrates' death.

ARISTOPHANES

The earliest surviving writings on Socrates are attributed to the comic playwright Aristophanes (circa 448–385 BC). In his play *The Clouds*, Aristophanes parodied Socrates and his disciples, portraying the old sage (or wise person) as the leader of an airy, insubstantial school whose students' heads were in the clouds as they discussed vague, lofty matters that bore little relation to daily reality down here on earth. Aristophanes used clouds as a metaphor for Socrates' contemplation of vague, fluffy ideas that floated far above the practical problems of life on the ground and in the streets. *The Clouds* doesn't shed much light on Socrates' life, but it does show that the philosopher, while still living, was prominent enough of a figure to be worthy of a popular playwright's mockery.

PLATO

Plato (circa 428–348 BC), one of Socrates' disciples who later become a much-acclaimed philosopher in

Ancient fragments of a papyrus inscribed with verses from Aristophanes'
Peace appear above. Aristophanes (represented by the bust) was a Greek
playwright of comedies. *Peace* was first performed in 421 BC, following a
decade-long war between Athens and Sparta. *Peace* is an antiwar play in
which a Greek patriot journeys to Mount Olympus to persuade Zeus to
finally end the miseries of war.

his own right, wrote dialogues (a kind of philosophical debate play) in which Socrates was a central figure. In these works, Plato depicted his former teacher engaged in hypothetical (or imaginary) conversations with students, friends, and well-known Athenian leaders of the time. It is hard to determine whether these dialogues depict an authentic Socrates or whether they serve as a mouthpiece for Plato's own philosophical thoughts.

The uncertainty arises because Plato's dialogues were written after Socrates' death. Plato's depiction of Socrates may have been more of a recollection of memories than his teacher's actual thoughts. In addition, Plato had his own ambitions as a philosopher, and these may have colored his portrayal of Socrates. Plato's early works, especially *Apology*, *Crito*, and *Phaedo*, are generally regarded as accurate showcases of Socrates' philosophies. Plato's later dialogues, however, are viewed as his own theories presented through the utterances of a Socrates treated more as a literary figure than a historical one.

XENOPHON

Though Plato's works are thought to provide the most reliable information about Socrates' life and thought, the military general Xenophon's (circa 433–355 BC) dialogues are perhaps more useful in providing an understanding of Socrates' fate. A former disciple of Socrates', Xenophon was the last contemporary biographer of the philosopher whose works on the thinker have survived.

Xenophon's dialogues were released a few decades after Socrates was sentenced to death. They were intended to preserve and defend the memory and wisdom of Socrates against the critics who continued to condemn him long after his execution. *Memorabilia of Socrates* and *Apology* depict Socrates' trial and the last days of his life. There are suggestions that Xenophon may have written *Memorabilia* and *Apology* partly to ease the guilt he felt for his own role in Socrates' condemnation. As will be seen later, when Socrates was on trial before the Athenian court, the close relationship between Xenophon and Socrates strongly influenced the ruling that would end the life of the general's much-respected master.

FAMILY AND EDUCATION

Socrates was born around 470 BC in a village on the slopes of Mount Lycabettus, which was about a

This first-century-AD Roman stone carving depicts a woman giving birth (*center*) assisted by two midwives. In ancient Greece, the delivery of babies was often handled by women, usually female relatives, neighbors, or servants, rather than male doctors. Some women specialized in childbirth and drew upon years of labor experience and great familiarity with medical lore. These women were often given the title *maia*, or midwife. A birthing chair like the one seen above was often used during labor. One or two women would stand behind it and hold the expectant mother still, while the midwife would kneel to deliver the baby.

twenty-minute walk to Athens. Today, Athens is the capital of Greece, but back then it was a powerful and independent city-state, a small nation unto itself. Socrates was raised in a household that was considered to be neither wealthy nor poor. His father, Sophroniscus, worked with stone, either as a stonecutter or a

sculptor. When Socrates was old enough, his father taught him the stoneworkers' trade.

Socrates' mother, Phaenarete, worked as a midwife (a woman who helps other women give birth). In ancient Greece, women worked outside the home only if their financial or marital circumstances made it necessary. Most of these women worked either because they were single or widowed and struggling to make ends meet. Sophroniscus's work probably supported the family well enough, so it's a mystery why Socrates' mother also held a job.

Socrates is thought to have received an elementary education typical among male Athenian youths at the time, including the study of music, literature, and gymnastics. He also received extensive instruction in geometry, astronomy, and natural science, which was unusual. There is evidence that he was a pupil of the fifth-century philosopher Archelaus, who in turn studied under Anaxagoras (circa 500–428 BC), a Greek philosopher who was born in Asia Minor but moved to Athens. Anaxagoras was primarily concerned with cosmology (study of the heavens) and theories of motion and creation, including the origins and development of matter and living things.

Socrates' early interest in this kind of scientific investigation eventually gave way in his adult life to an almost exclusive focus on moral and ethical inquiry—what is a good life, and how does one live it? Plato's and Xenophon's dialogues indicate that Socrates spent almost no time pondering physics and cosmology, apparently considering them unimportant to questions about human nature, moral development, and destiny.

MARRIED LIFE

When he was fifty years old, Socrates married a woman named Xanthippe, and they had three sons. Xanthippe carried an infant in her arms to the prison cell where she said good-bye to Socrates. This indicates that she was probably considerably younger than Socrates, as she was still of childbearing age when her seventy-one-year-old husband was condemned to death.

There are conflicting accounts as to whether Socrates and Xanthippe's household was a happy one. Some stories maintain that Socrates loved his wife for her intellect—she was said to be the only person who could get the better of her husband in a debate. Other tales paint Xanthippe as a bit of a bully and a nag. Her frustration and anger may have arisen from Socrates' decision to spend his days preaching on the streets for free instead of working at a paying job.

Several theories exist concerning how Socrates supported himself and his family with no earnings. He refused to take money from his students, a practice for which he criticized his philosophical predecessors. He may have survived on a little bit of money that his father had left him, or he may have lived off the wealth from Xanthippe's side of the family. He probably received some gifts of money and food from his well-heeled disciples, despite his objections to the practice.

Nothing in Socrates' early life gave any indication that he would eventually give up his relatively comfortable life as a skilled tradesperson to become a penniless philosopher who walked the streets of Athens loudly criticizing strangers about their moral condition. However, this stonecutter's son would become one of the world's greatest and most influential thinkers, shaping Western notions of law, ethics, and philosophy for ages to come.

SOLDIER FOR ATHENS

As a young man, Socrates was not always poor. Before he became a teacher, who perhaps sometimes reluctantly accepted the generosity of his friends and family, Socrates earned his keep as a stonecutter. On

several occasions, he also served as a soldier in the Athenian army.

Though Athens enjoyed a peaceful period during Socrates' young adulthood and into his middle age, the city-state did engage in a few minor military campaigns. Athens had a large civilian militia in which citizens were on call to fight if and when they were needed. After serving in battles, soldiers returned to civilian life.

Socrates was called to duty on at least two campaigns, the first when he was in his thirties, against the city-state Samos, and the second when he was

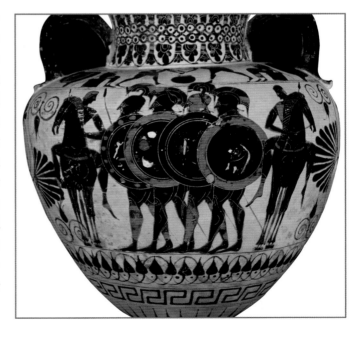

Greek hoplites and horsemen gather together in advance of a battle in this sixth-century-BC amphora made by the so-called Princeton Painter. An amphora is an ancient Greek jar or vase with a large oval body, a narrow rounded neck, and two handles. The Greek word for weapon is *hoplon*, so "hoplite" translates as something like "man at arms" or "armed man."

nearly forty, in the battle against the city-state Potidaea. He fought as a hoplite, or a foot soldier. Hoplites had to supply their own armor, so people of the middle class were generally the only ones who were wealthy enough to be able to serve in this division. Socrates did not fight in the cavalry, which was made up of aristocrats (who had to supply their own horses, a major expense), nor did he fight with the poor in the lightly armed infantry. At some point in his life, it appears Socrates did have considerable money. The popular depiction of him as the impoverished philosopher is not an accurate portrayal of his financial situation during the whole of his life.

When Socrates served as a hoplite in the fight against Potidaea in 432 BC, he shared his living quarters with a young man named Alcibiades (circa 450–404 BC). The two formed the kind of friendship that often develops between soldiers engaged in warfare, but their bond became especially close when Socrates saved the life of his comrade, a brave act that would later come back to haunt him. During a fierce battle, Alcibiades was wounded and fell to the ground. Socrates stood over his friend and protected him from further harm, despite the danger to himself.

Little did Socrates know that his heroic service in the battle at Potidaea would contribute to his death by execution three decades later. What was initially celebrated as a beautiful friendship born of the battlefield later became one of the chief pieces of evidence in the trial against him.

PHILOSOPHICAL INFLUENCES

The word "philosophy" comes from the Greek words *philos* (love) and *sofia* (wisdom), so "philosophy" literally means "love of wisdom." How Socrates supported his family, and at what point in his life he gave up his stonecutters' tools, backbreaking days in the sun, and a steady income in order to devote himself to a penniless life in search of wisdom is uncertain. But Socrates was probably introduced to philosophy by his teacher Archelaus, who encouraged him to read the works of early natural philosophers. Socrates may have had contact with some of these thinkers or their students when they passed through Athens. Today, these early thinkers are known as the pre-Socratic philosophers.

The Pre-Socratics

The pre-Socratics departed from earlier sages (wise men) by trying to understand the world through logic and reason rather than with the help of religion

The sixth-century-BC pre-Socratic Greek philosopher Pythagoras appears in this 1865 French engraving entitled *The School of Pythagoras*. He can be seen in the center, standing apart from his students who circle him and gesturing to illustrate a point. Pythagoras was a mathematician, musical theorist, spiritual mystic, and philosopher who founded a society in the Greek colony of Croton, in modern-day southern Italy. There he instructed his students in mathematical, spiritual, and moral matters.

and mythology. These philosophers turned their focus to the natural world and made claims about life, Earth, and the universe, based on scientific observations and mathematics. One of the leading thinkers in this group was Pythagoras, for whom the Pythagorean branch of pre-Socratic philosophy is named.

The pre-Socratics were usually Greeks who lived outside Athens, were sometimes educated in Egypt and Persia (modern-day Iran, where the study of math and science was far advanced), and traveled around the Mediterranean islands teaching their ideas. The pre-Socratics must have sparked Socrates' interest in philosophy, as they were the most famous and respected philosophers when he was a boy. At some point, he must have listened to what they had to say when they passed through Athens.

The Sophists

As a young man, Socrates also encountered another group of early thinkers called the Sophists. The Sophists were given the nickname "wisdom-sellers" because they traveled around the Mediterranean offering to teach subjects such as rhetoric (the study of argument) and logic to anyone who was willing to pay for the instruction.

Socrates disagreed with many of the Sophists' ways of doing things. The Sophists' arguably hypocritical practice of demanding money while urging people to reconsider their values inspired Socrates' refusal to charge his students. He felt he had a vocation or mission to spread virtue. And this vocation was a contribution to society, not a moneymaking scheme. If he had to sacrifice a comfortable life to this noble mission, so be it.

Socrates also disagreed with the Sophists' approach to rhetoric as a tool for persuasion. The Sophists believed that for the sake of training a student's argumentative skills, the student should take a position in a debate and argue that position tirelessly, regardless of whether the position is right or wrong or whether the student really believes what he or she is arguing. Related to this, one of the leading Sophists, Protagoras, believed that there was no such thing as absolute and universal truth or falsehood. If something seemed true to one person, then it was true for that person. If the same thing seemed false to another person, then it was false for that person. Socrates believed that truth was both sacred and objective (not something that changed from situation to situation, or from person to person). He felt that truth should never be compromised for the sake of argument, or for anything else.

Nevertheless, in later life, Socrates was often labeled a Sophist by the Athenians, including by his own students and followers. He was similar to the Sophists in that he had little or no interest in questions relating to metaphysics, cosmology, or the physical world. Both Socrates and the Sophists were concerned mainly with ethics. They are remembered for their methods of questioning ethical beliefs, rather than providing ethical "answers" or a set of philosophical absolutes. And both were more interested in breaking down other people's moral beliefs and ideas by revealing their flaws than in providing their listeners with an alternative, improved moral system by which to live. Like the Sophists, Socrates did not always offer clear guidelines on truth and virtue. Instead, he acted as a moral critic who shook the confidence of his audience in the truth of their popularly held opinions.

The Emergence of Moral Philosophy

Despite Socrates' ethical and philosophical differences with its practitioners, Sophism is the branch of philosophy that appears to have had the most influence in shaping Socrates' own ideas. While the Pythagoreans devoted their energy to understanding the mysteries of the universe through mysticism, mathematics, and numbers and scientific observation, Sophists sought to understand the world through the lens of morality.

The Sophists believed that people should devote themselves to the quest to define what it means to be good or virtuous and that they should use this new knowledge and understanding to change their personal conduct. They didn't believe that philosophy should exist only to spark discussion, but rather that the ideas and conclusions that come out of philosophical debate should be put to practical use to improve the lives and behaviors of individuals and their communities.

One of Socrates' most cherished wise sayings was "know thyself," which he may have read as an inscription on the Oracle of Delphi. Socrates seized on this idea that in order to do good in the world, one must start by examining oneself. The origin of the expression "know thyself" is fundamental to the story of Socrates' lifelong inquiry into his own moral health and that of his fellow Athenians.

2 | A PHILOSOPHER IS BORN

By the time he was thirty years old, Socrates had devoted his life exclusively to the pursuit of truth. A single trip taken by his friend Chaerephon at this time set Socrates on a philosophical quest that would last throughout the rest of his life. The trip Chaerephon made was to the Oracle at Delphi, a sacred shrine dedicated to Apollo, the Greek god of music and the arts.

Ancient Greeks were polytheistic, meaning they worshipped many gods and goddesses, not just one. From across the entire Greek world, which stretched into Asia Minor and southern Italy, people traveled to pay their respects and get answers to questions they asked the divine oracles at numerous sacred spots scattered throughout the Greek territories. One of the most visited shrines was

This larger-than-life-size bronze statue was discovered in 1972 in the Bay of Riace, Calabria, Italy. It is thought to have been made by the famous Greek sculptor Phidias in the fifth century BC. The sculpture may have originally been a votive at the shrine of Delphi. Votive statues were placed throughout Delphi in order to please the gods, thank the oracle for advice, or commemorate military victories. Phidias was most famous for his sculpture of Athena in the Parthenon and his Zeus in the Temple of Olympia.

at Delphi. It was here that what Socrates believed to be a divine message was delivered, one that would guide him throughout the remainder of his life.

UNDERSTANDING THE ORACLE'S MESSAGE

Chaerephon went to Delphi with a particular question in mind. He asked the oracle whether there was anybody wiser than Socrates. The oracle declared that Socrates was the wisest man of all time. At first, when Chaerephon reported the oracle's reply to his friend, the modest Socrates was bewildered. He was absolutely sure that he was not wise, much less the wisest of all,

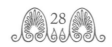

and wondered why the all-knowing oracle would make such a false statement. He was determined to understand the exact meaning of the prophecy, and he asked himself question after question until he arrived at a conclusion that made sense to him.

Socrates was absolutely sure that he was not yet wise and wanted to uncover what the oracle meant. By asking himself question after question, he arrived at a clearer meaning underlying the oracle's mysterious words: Socrates was the wisest person precisely because he alone knew and admitted to himself that he was not wise. The only way in which he was wiser than other people was that he knew something about himself that they didn't know about themselves—that he was an ignorant man who knew absolutely nothing except the fact of his own ignorance.

At the time of Chaerephon's pilgrimage to Delphi, Socrates was about thirty years old. It is unclear what the status of his career was at this point—whether he was already steeped in teaching and philosophical inquiry, or whether the oracle's proclamation prompted his abandonment of stonework for a life dedicated to pursuits of the mind. What is known is that the oracle's declaration played a major role in Socrates' life. It served as the inspiration for his famous approach to philosophical inquiry—the so-called Socratic method.

THE SOCRATIC METHOD

Unlike many of the philosophers who are well known and studied today, Socrates did not have a core set of beliefs that he taught and sought to explain. Socrates' actual ideas were not his greatest legacy. In fact, little of his actual philosophy has come down to us. What did make him famous, however, was his method of

The Oracle at Delphi

The Oracle at Delphi was constructed around 1400 BC, on the slope of Mount Parnassus, located west of Athens. It was devoted to Apollo, the god of music and the arts, and built around a sacred spring in Delphi, which the Greeks considered to be the center of the world. People traveled from far and wide to present their offerings of gold and get their questions answered by the Pythia, a priestess of Apollo. The Pythia had to be at least fifty years old and was required to live in seclusion near the temple. On the day she gave oracles, usually once a month, she would undergo a cleansing ritual that ancient Greeks believed put her into a trance. Priests were present at Delphi to translate her prophecies to visitors.

Government leaders would send gifts to be placed at the temple in exchange for Apollo's protection of their city-states. As a result, Delphi eventually became a showplace for marvelous art and other treasures. In the fourth century AD, after Greece converted to Christianity, all oracles around the Mediterranean were silenced. Over time, looters raided and stole the treasures housed at the spots once considered sacred by the ancient Greeks.

The ruins of the Temple of Apollo remain standing on the slopes of Mount Parnassus, more than 2,300 years after the columns were erected. The temple was first built in the seventh century BC, but it was destroyed and rebuilt twice. It featured a peristasis—a colonnade, or outer hall formed by columns—that surrounded the temple. The Delphi priestess would pass through these columns, enter this temple, sit at her tripod, and fall into a trance in which she answered the questions of worshippers.

questioning, which he developed as he puzzled over the oracle's prophecy. The Socratic method was designed to gain understanding of difficult philosophical problems that did not necessarily have clear-cut answers. He believed that through the asking of a carefully constructed series of questions, a person could reach solid conclusions. At the very least, the questions could bring to the surface the confusions, contradictions, and errors at the heart of the conventional ethical beliefs of most Athenians.

Socrates compared these question-and-answer dialogues to the work of a midwife. He said that his questions gave birth to his debate partner's definitions and ideas. Socrates himself never took a position. Rather, he simply exposed the errors of other people's conventional, unexamined assumptions and encouraged them to form a more correct view. In this way, Socrates aided the birth of other people's ideas, but the people who engaged in debates with him did most of the work by pushing their ideas to the surface in response to his questions.

The purpose of the Socratic method was to get people to raise ethical questions and come up with answers for themselves, rather than blindly accept the morality handed down to them by their political and religious leaders or by society. He wanted to shake people out of their belief that they already knew everything and had it all figured out. If he could make them confront the fact that they didn't know very much after all, they would then be better able to acquire real knowledge.

The Socratic method was a two-part process. Socrates would begin by pretending to know little about whatever was being discussed, asking questions of his pupils in order to learn something. Feeling flattered by Socrates' apparent respect for their intelligence and knowledge, and perhaps made a little overconfident as a result, they would often put forth positions that were built upon flawed premises. Socrates' volley of questions would soon expose his pupils' ignorance and force them to admit the error of their opinions. This is known as the destructive part of the process.

Having identified and rejected the flawed opinions, Socrates would then move to a second series of questions designed to make his pupils develop new, more thought-out opinions about the subject being discussed. This is known as the constructive part of the process. These improved opinions were usually the end result of Socrates' urging his students, through questions, to arrive at definitions of the subject being discussed, and thereby achieve knowledge.

Socrates believed that right conduct depended upon clear knowledge. For example, he believed that by defining virtue, we are better equipped to acquire virtue and become virtuous. Going even further, he felt that simply arriving at a definition for virtue was a virtue in itself. Socrates believed that virtue is knowledge and that knowledge is virtue. It follows that various kinds of things we label as virtues, such as justice, courage, self-control, and piety (respect for and obedience to the gods), are also forms of wisdom, or knowledge. The possession of these forms of wisdom makes one a virtuous person. He believed that if one knows what is good, one will do what is good.

Socrates referred to his method of truth-seeking as *elenchus*, which translates as "cross-examination." It gave rise in the Western world to a kind of philosophical inquiry known as dialectic—the arrival at truth by exposing one's idea to opposing positions and modifying it as a result of the debate. It was through the Socratic method that Socrates came to an understanding not only of the oracle's exalted prophecy but also other, more universal moral and ethical truths.

Though Socrates' visit to Delphi gave him a sense of purpose, it was a mixed blessing. All of Athens soon heard about the oracle's startling declaration. By the time he returned from the pilgrimage, probably a little puffed up with new self-confidence, Socrates found himself thrust into Athens's limelight and discovered the double-edged sword that can accompany fame. Although Socrates probably enjoyed suddenly having a large and enthusiastic audience, he also became a source of annoyance and an object of resentment, which eventually resulted in accusations by a powerful few who were determined to bring Socrates to ruin.

3 ATHENS'S RISE AND FALL

In order to understand Socrates' trial and execution, one must become familiar with the history and culture of fifth-century-BC Athens. For most of Socrates' life, Athens was at the forefront of Mediterranean culture, politics, and art. The city was vibrant with expressions of its citizens' patriotism and their extraordinary artistic and cultural contributions, which millennia later are still regarded with awe. Athenians built magnificent architectural monuments as gifts to the gods. A democratic leadership gave the people a voice, a right to opinions and self-expression, and an education to form these opinions.

This exciting, creative time in Athenian history is known as its golden age. Let's take a look back to a few years before Socrates was born to see how Athens's greatness came to be. The rise and fall of

Beginning in the twelfth century BC, Greek people began migrating from mainland Greece across the Aegean Sea toward Asia Minor, where they founded new colonies. At the dawn of the fifth century, Greek colonies in Asia Minor were under the thumb of the Persian Empire, which spread throughout half of Asia. Some of them revolted and sought the help of mainland Greek allies in their struggle against the Persian Empire, starting the Persian Wars. This map of fifth-century-BC Greece indicates the various Greek people who lived on the mainland and migrated to Asia Minor.

its fortunes are directly related to the twists of fate in Socrates' own life.

THE PERSIAN WARS AND ATHENS'S NEW DOMINANCE

The nation of Greece did not exist during Socrates' time. In ancient times, the country we now call Greece was a collection of more than 100 small, independent city-states, or poleis. Each polis functioned as a separate nation with its own government. Athens was the biggest city-state in the fifth century BC, with a population of 300,000 to 350,000 people. The citizens in each of these city-states swore allegiance only to their own polis, and the local customs and traditions were very different within each polis. However, the citizens of the Greek city-states shared a common written and spoken language, and they would join together for the Olympic Games and sometimes to fight a common enemy. This arrangement had been in place for about three centuries before Socrates' time.

Socrates came of age during one of the few times in Athens's history that was marked by an extended period of peace. Greece's ancient history was one of almost constant warfare, and a persistent enemy was Persia (an empire centered in modern-day Iran). Fifth-century-BC

Three runners compete in a footrace in this sixth-century-BC Greek amphora. The competition depicted is thought to represent the Panathenaic Games. Part of a large religious festival known as the Panathenaia, these games were held in Athens every four years. Modeled on the Olympic Games but far less important, the first Panathenaic Games took place in 566 BC and included music and poetry competitions. Athletic events included boxing, wrestling, chariot racing, and the pentathlon.

Persia had an empire that spanned much of the Middle East, Asia Minor, and central Asia, including some Greek colonies to the north and east of Athens. The Persian Empire had a very strong military that was used both to defend its borders and extend its territory. In 499 BC,

Darius I, king of ancient Persia, ruled from 522 to 486 BC. Under the war-like Darius, the borders of the Persian Empire reached their farthest extent. He came to control the Greek cities in Asia Minor, which were forced to pay him high tributes in the form of cash and goods. When Athens sought to defend these Greek cities, Darius led the Persians into war against almost the whole of Greece. He came close to conquering the Greek world but was finally defeated by the Athenians in 490 BC. The above image, from the Frieze of Archers, depicts Darius's archers, shown in ceremonial dress. The frieze once adorned Darius's royal palace at Susa (in modern-day Iran), one of the oldest cities in the world.

the Persian army attempted to conquer more Greek city-states. With Athens at the helm, the city-states brought under Persian control began to rebel, beginning a conflict known as the Persian Wars (circa 499–479 BC).

The Athenians led an alliance of Greek city-states that eventually defeated the Persians after a twenty-year war, with a final naval battle at Salamis in 480 BC, resulting in the triumph of a badly outnumbered Athenian fleet. In 479 BC, a Spartan king led the Greek allies in the Battle of Plataea, leading to the final retreat of the Persian forces. The allied Greek city-states declared victory, and Athens was praised as the Persian Wars' ultimate victor.

THE AGE OF PERICLES

"Future ages will wonder at us, as the present age wonders at us now." This was the accurate prediction of the statesman Pericles (circa 495–429 BC), which was uttered as he contemplated the great undertakings into which he would soon lead Athenians. Pericles, who was at the forefront of Athens's golden age, ruled from 460 BC to 431 BC. He was determined to go down in history as the statesman most responsible for Athens's long-lasting greatness. He eventually succeeded in this lofty goal.

A Roman copy of a fifth-century-BC Greek original bust of Pericles appears at left. He is shown wearing a Corinthian helmet, which was among the most popular helmets during the Archaic and early classical periods in Greece. They were usually made of bronze, covered the head and neck, and included openings for the eyes and mouth. The helmet on this bust may signify Pericles' status as a *strategos*, or a commander of the army. Pericles served as a strategos during the Peloponnesian War (431–404 BC), a war between Sparta and Athens and their allies that resulted in a victory for Sparta and its control of much of the Greek lands once dominated by Athens.

Pericles was from a wealthy, aristocratic family. Like most young men, he started his military career as an ordinary soldier but rose rapidly to the post of statesman-general. Aside from his family connections, Pericles' sharp intellect and powerful personality helped him rise in the political world. Pericles' charisma and persuasive speeches won over voters in election after election, and his civic proposals gained the support of his Assembly colleagues. As the strongest advocate for reforms and progress during the fifth century BC, Pericles is considered

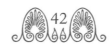

the visionary of Athens's golden age, an era of unparalleled achievement that may not have been possible without him.

GOLDEN AGE ATHENIAN CULTURE

The Greek city-states were among the first societies to foster the development of an intellectual class. In Athens's case, this was partly due to the recent installation of direct democracy, the first such political system in the world. Rather than citizens electing officials to represent them, as in a representative democracy like that of the United States, Athens's voting citizens all had a direct voice in government at meetings that were open to the public.

Because the individual was so important in a direct democracy, and because the average citizen had an immediate influence upon public policy and decision-making, Pericles believed it was important to develop a cultured, educated, and intelligent citizenry. As a result, Pericles advanced the idea that it was important for governments to invest in the arts.

During Athens's golden age, Pericles encouraged the work of scientists, musicians, and poets—almost anybody who had a talent to share. He supported talented artists with lavish government funding and encouraged their input on civic projects. One of the most monumental public projects during his reign was the building of the Parthenon, which was a temple dedicated to the goddess Athena.

The Acropolis had been damaged in the Persian Wars and the Athenians were able to rebuild it at the

The Greek sculptor Phidias is seen showing the frieze he created for the Parthenon, which was under construction, in this nineteenth-century painting by Sir Lawrence Alma-Tadema. Historians have no proof that Phidias actually created any of the sculptures housed in the Parthenon. It is believed that much of the art may have instead been created by Phidias's pupils.

same time the Parthenon was under construction, giving further evidence of the city's abundant wealth at that time. It is rumored that Socrates contributed his skills as a stonemason during these rebuilding efforts. In addition, one of the most talented sculptors of the ancient world, Phidias (circa 500–432 BC), lived during this time and constructed the celebrated statue of Zeus, which was designated as one of the Seven Wonders of the Ancient World.

Pericles' artistic initiatives weren't designed only to beautify the city. Political considerations were also driving forces behind the building of these monuments. Flush with victory after the Persian Wars, Pericles wanted to create impressive displays of Athenian power, and he used these projects to show off Athens's might and riches. For example, the sculptures of the Parthenon served as artistic propaganda that told of Athens's military victories. The grandeur of the temple alone broadcast the superiority of Athens to all who passed by.

The golden age was a great time to be living in Athens—as long as you were a male citizen. Women were not permitted to attend school, participate in politics or vote, and were generally confined to the home. Male Athenian citizens had more free time to enjoy the grandeur and cultural richness of their city, due in part to slavery. Despite Athens's progressive experiments in democracy, it didn't have qualms about using slave labor or giving citizens certain rights and freedoms denied to others living in their midst. At least one-quarter of Athens's population was made up of slaves, who were usually prisoners of war. Despite its reliance on slavery and its denial of citizenship to some residents, Athens enjoyed relative peace and prosperity

Slaves

Perhaps the worst fate in the golden age of Athens was captivity and enslavement. Slaves made up a large portion of Athens's population, but they were not granted any of the rights of citizens. Many were forced to mine silver. These slaves spent long, dark days in dangerous underground tunnels. Most slaves were prisoners captured in battle, and, in some cases, victims of kidnappings in other city-states or throughout the Mediterranean islands. The slave was often paid for his or her services and could eventually buy his or her freedom and become a metic, or resident alien. However, metics still did not enjoy the same rights as Athenian citizens.

Though they were not treated very well, slaves provided the foundation for the glories of Athens's golden age. Their labor built the city's world-famous and enduring architectural marvels, and, in an indirect way, slaves also helped establish the philosophical underpinnings of the golden age. Ironically, Athens would not have become the progressive society that it was without the contribution of slave labor, for this afforded the intellectuals the time and leisure to think about public ethics and morality. Socrates, though a harsh critic of Athenian society's morals, never questioned the institution of slavery.

A channel of a silver washing station from an ancient silver mine in Lavrion, Greece, a port town on the Attiki Peninsula, appears above. In the holes, or cups, visible in the channel, silver would be washed and extracted. These ruins are thought to represent the oldest mining facilities in the world. The Lavrion silver mines helped Athens finance the wars and the building of the Acropolis and other monuments of its golden age.

A modern watercolor by Peter Connolly depicts a scene from the Battle of Salamis, fought in 480 BC. Though the Persian fleet far outnumbered the ships of the Greek alliance, which included Athens, Sparta, and other city-states, the Greeks won the battle through hand-to-hand combat, well-crafted ships, and swimming expertise.

during this period. The citizens seemed happy with and trusting of their leaders. As a result, culture flourished, allowing a figure as eccentric as Socrates to emerge as one of Athens's most respected, if not most well-liked, thinkers.

THE DELIAN LEAGUE AND PERICLES' CORRUPTION

After its triumph over Persia at the Battle of Salamis, Athens founded the Delian League with many of its city-state allies. The league was a collective security alliance that offered each city-state the protection of its Greek allies from foreign invasion. Sparta was the only major Greek city-state that refused to take part in this joint safety net. Athens collected taxes from the league's member states and set aside this money for any necessary military campaigns in the future. In its early stages, the alliance was very active. It fought the Persians in their remaining strongholds and eventually drove them out of the Aegean and from the coasts of Asia Minor. As the Persian threat receded, however, the allies grew impatient with the constant need to contribute to the defense fund. They were no longer convinced it was necessary.

While the other city-states continued to add to the fund, Athens stopped paying its share of the taxes, contributing nothing to the league's treasury for decades. In fact, the fund was used to pay for local initiatives. Pericles dipped into the defense treasury to finance city-improvement projects, including the construction of the Parthenon.

By the end of his reign, Pericles had harmed Athens nearly as much as he had helped it. His costly projects and dishonest financial dealings are blamed for causing a chain of events that eventually brought down the greatest glory of golden age Athens, its democratic system. Pericles' tragic flaw may have been that he lacked foresight. His plans for improving Athens didn't take into consideration a long-term view of the future. He chose not to consider how Athens's neighbors would react to the city's great show of riches, a wealth built upon theft from its allies.

Ancient Sparta was a highly militaristic society, and its male members were trained from birth to become soldiers. Any newborn male thought to be weak or sickly was left to die in the mountains. Those who were spared began military training at the age of seven. When young Spartan men turned twenty, they became hoplites, or foot soldiers, bearing helmet, shield, sword, spear, and armor, like the sixth-century-BC bronze Spartan warrior seen at right.

PELOPONNESIAN WAR

Throughout Athens's golden age, the city's great enemy, Sparta, which held alliances with most of the small city-states not affiliated with Athens, was growing more and more anxious about Athens's astounding power and wealth. In 460 BC, Sparta launched an attack against its rival. What

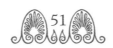

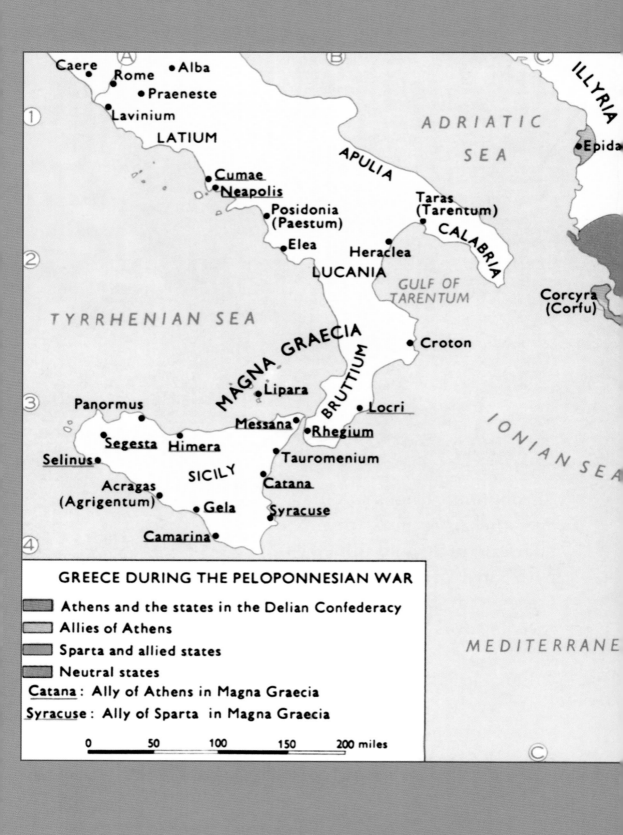

Caere • • Alba
• Rome
• Praeneste
• Lavinium
LATIUM

ILLYRIA

ADRIATIC
SEA

• Epida

APULIA

• Cumae
• Neapolis
Posidonia
(Paestum)
• Elea

Taras
(Tarentum)

CALABRIA

Heraclea

LUCANIA

GULF OF
TARENTUM

Corcyra
(Corfu)

TYRRHENIAN SEA

MAGNA GRAECIA

• Croton

Panormus •

Lipara

BRUTTIUM

• Locri

Messana •
• Rhegium

IONIAN SEA

• Segesta Himera •

Selinus •

Tauromenium

SICILY

• Catana

Acragas
(Agrigentum)

• Gela

Syracuse

Camarina •

GREECE DURING THE PELOPONNESIAN WAR

Athens and the states in the Delian Confederacy
Allies of Athens
Sparta and allied states
Neutral states

Catana : Ally of Athens in Magna Graecia

Syracuse : Ally of Sparta in Magna Graecia

0   50   100   150   200 miles

MEDITERRANE

THRACE

MACEDONIA

Amphipolis

Thasos

Aegospotami

Byzantium

PHRYGIA
(GALATIA)

Olynthus

Lemnos

Troy (Ilium)

US

THESSALY

Lesbos

Mytilene

PERSIAN

EMPIRE

BOEOTIA

Euboea

Chios

IONIA

Ephesus

Leuctra

Thebes

AEGEAN SEA

Corinth

Athens
Piraeus

Samos

Miletus

Elis

Olympia

Argos

Aegina

PELOPONNESUS

Cyclades

MES-
SENIA

Pylus

Sparta

LACONIA

Cnidus

Sphacteria

Melos

Rhodes

Cythera

SEA

This map depicts the Greek territories at the time of the Peloponnesian
War, which began in 431 BC. Angered by and jealous of Athens's power,
wealth, and arrogance, Sparta and its allies invaded Attica (the entire territory of the Athenian city-state, of which the city of Athens was a part)
and began burning Athenian crops. Sparta would eventually attack the
city of Athens and force the city-state's surrender in 404 BC, ending
the Athenian golden age. This map indicates the territories controlled
by Athens, Sparta, their respective allies, and neutral Greek city-states.

followed was fifteen years of combat between the two city-states.

It had been decades since the allied Greek territories had engaged in any serious battles with Persia, and many city-states no longer saw the Persian Empire as a major threat. There was a growing movement among the city-states of the Delian League to withdraw from the alliance and stop paying taxes to Athens for protection that was no longer needed. As the city-states voiced their intention to drop out, Athens used its strong naval fleet—paid for with Delian League funds—to flex its muscle. For example, when leaders of Miletus told Athens about the city-state's intention to stop paying taxes to the league, Athens sent its navy to destroy the city.

By 431 BC, Sparta had formed a new alliance of city-states that were angered by Athens's abuse of power and wanted to topple it from its dominant perch. Thus began a series of battles collectively known as the Peloponnesian War, which was ultimately won by Sparta.

War was not Athens's only woe, however. Under Pericles' leadership, the Athenians adopted a defensive strategy, in which their navy harassed the Spartans with quick raids, while their army and citizens retreated behind the city walls and refused to engage the Spartans' stronger land forces. Due to the overcrowding that resulted, Athens fell victim to a mysterious plague that eventually claimed at least 25 percent of its population. Pericles, along with his entire family, died from this plague in 429 BC. Without a strong leadership, Athens was in no position to continue battling the tireless and fierce Spartans.

The final battle in the Peloponnesian War occurred in 404 BC. Athens was besieged and forced to surrender. Upon Athens's defeat, Sparta immediately installed a group of Athenian nobles, known as the Thirty Tyrants, to rule over the city-state. The Thirty Tyrants embarked on a reign of terror. Led by Critias, a former associate of Socrates', they executed 1,500 of their opponents and confiscated their property. Stunned by this unprecedented violence, the pro-democratic Athenians fled into exile. They organized a resistance and retook part of the city, as all-out war broke out. Sparta stepped in to declare an amnesty (an official declaration of peace and forgiveness) and restored democracy in 403 BC. Though the Athenians had regained their government, the Pericles era of Athenian intellectualism, achievement, and power had ended. Athenians were bitter and demoralized, and their city would never again enjoy a period of such dominance, influence, and creative flowering.

4 THE GADFLY OF ATHENS

In many ways, Socrates was a man of contradictions. In his personal life, he was described as an ascetic (a sort of hermit who chooses to live in poverty and a state of self-denial). He sacrificed material comforts for his intellectual pursuits.

However, there is evidence that Socrates may not have been as modest as his shabby appearance would indicate. While he downplayed the wisdom that the Oracle at Delphi had celebrated him for, he considered its utterance to be a message from the gods. He felt set apart and under divine orders to encourage others to think about philosophical matters. Socrates used this divine calling as an excuse for not participating in civic affairs that lay outside his philosophical pursuits.

And so I go my way, obedient to the god, and make inquisition into the wisdom of any one, whether citizen or stranger, who appears to be wise; and if he is not wise, then in vindication of the oracle I show him that he is not wise; and this occupation quite absorbs me, and I have no time to give either to any public matter of interest or to any concern of my own . . . (as quoted in *The Republic and Other Works*).

By his own admission, Socrates seems to have delighted in highlighting other people's lack of wisdom, thereby proving his own. He also seemed to relish the fact that he had been chosen by the gods and set apart from other men and women to pursue his divine "occupation." He remained dedicated to this divine purpose throughout his life. The fact that he could be very abrasive in his approach to this calling would ultimately land him in hot water.

RUFFLING FEATHERS AND GAINING A FOLLOWING

Socrates felt it was his duty to share the Delphi oracle's revelation that each and every human being was

hopelessly ignorant (or uninformed and unknowledge-able). The agora, or marketplace, was the place to which he took this harsh message. Athenians became the targets of Socrates' relentless method of question-ing, which was used to underscore their ignorance.

As people went about their daily business in the agora, Socrates felt it was his duty to engage those whom he encountered, asking them about their moral beliefs. He would use his roundabout Socratic method to reveal the flaws or weaknesses in his opponent's position and usually win the debates. He would take his debater's statements and question the validity and logic behind their premises. Usually his opponent would end up retracting (taking back) his statements or rethinking the premises that sup-ported them. Often, Socrates drew a crowd of eager listeners when he was engaged in these types of philosophical contests. He had a huge following of pupils in Athens, made up of curious young minds, leaders in the making, and men with lots of power and money.

Socrates was not trying to be mean-spirited in his attacks upon people's logic and beliefs. He just believed that if a person had come upon a good understanding of morality, it was his or her responsi-bility to share it with the community and convince

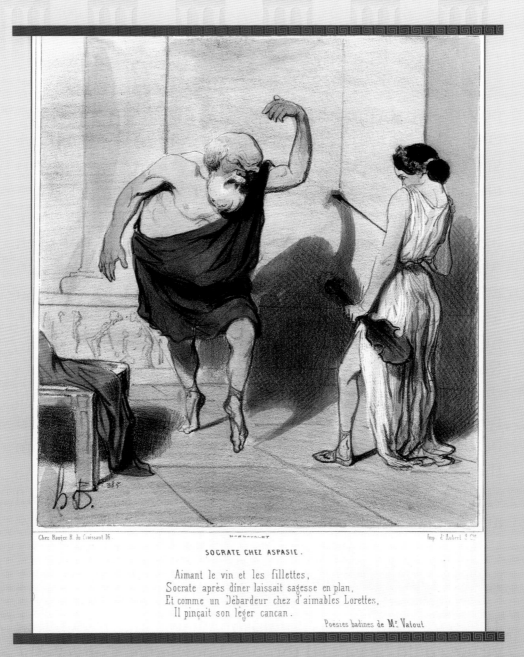

SOCRATE CHEZ ASPASIE.

Aimant le vin et les fillettes,
Socrate après dîner laissait sagesse en plan,
Et comme un Débardeur chez d'aimables Lorettes,
Il pinçait son léger cancan.

Poésies badines de Mr. Vatout

A sense of Socrates' free-spirited nature and unkempt appearance is conveyed in this nineteenth-century lithograph by Honoré Daumier. Socrates is dancing before Aspasia, a fifth-century-BC teacher, writer, and philosopher. Born in Miletus, Aspasia moved to Athens and founded a school for the education of the daughters of wealthy families. Highly educated and brilliant, Aspasia is credited with influencing leading classical philosophers, including Socrates, Plato, Xenophon, Cicero, Plutarch, and Athenaeus.

community members of its truth and value. Obviously not everybody took to Socrates' aggressive style of teaching, nor did they want to accept his claim that they were merely ignorant beings.

Socrates was well aware that his relentless questioning was not always appreciated. He even called himself Athens's "gadfly," which means a person who persistently pesters others through criticism, like a fly that annoys with buzzing and biting. Ultimately, however, he didn't care what others thought about him. Notorious for his unattractive appearance, he is often depicted in sculptures and paintings as having a pug nose and stocky frame. He was not in the habit of bathing or shaving. His round stomach stuck out from the loose robes he wore, and he walked around the agora barefoot. Socrates was considered a real oddball among the refined and cultured Athenians of his time.

RIGHT AND WRONG

The core of Socrates' philosophy was his belief that virtue could be gained through knowledge. Conversely, he believed that a person who does wrong is simply lacking in knowledge and acting out of ignorance. People do not do wrong on purpose. This is why Socrates chose to devote his life to educating his fellow

Was Socrates Mentally Ill?

Today, some mental health experts believe that Socrates may have suffered from mental illness. It was common for him to stand in contemplation in a catatonic state (motionless and expressionless), in which he would be as still as a statue, and would remain in that position for hours. This is a symptom of a type of mental disorder known as schizophrenia, which affects the body's motor system, so that a sort of stupor, trance, or frozen rigidity strikes the sufferer. A less severe diagnosis is that he may have had a form of epilepsy, which causes sufferers to stare into space, unaware of their surroundings, for anywhere from several minutes to a few hours.

Socrates was not completely unaware of his tendency to "space out." In fact, he may have relished these episodes. At his trial, Socrates referred to his daemon, a sort of supernatural guiding spirit. He claimed that this daemon warned him of events that were potentially disastrous and urged him either to take or refrain from a certain action in order to avoid trouble. This is not unlike the voices that some schizophrenics say they hear, often alerting them to imaginary dangers and threats.

In ancient times, people believed that diseases such as epilepsy were of divine origin. Their victims, the ancients believed, were inhabited by a divine force and, therefore, possessed mysterious and extraordinary powers. The slightly arrogant and self-important Socrates probably didn't mind being diagnosed with such a condition.

Socrates converses with one of the nine Muses in this second-century-BC Roman sarcophagus. A sarcophagus is a coffin that often bears carvings related to the life of the dead person. Plato claims that Socrates believed that locusts were once humans who became so enchanted by the music that came into the world after the birth of the Muses that they began to sing constantly, without stopping to eat or drink and eventually died. The Muses took pity on the singers and turned them into locusts, creatures that could "sing" continuously from birth to death.

citizens. If he taught Athenians through the posing of moral questions designed to make them examine their moral systems, then they would eventually gain the knowledge needed to lead more moral lives. They would learn how to do right in every situation.

Socrates believed that although people did not mean to do harm, their ignorance nevertheless fueled bad deeds. His lifelong quest to define goodness and truth was undertaken in the belief that if a person could define what was wrong, then he or she would know how to act morally. In the same way, if a person knew what was right, he or she would choose to avoid doing wrong. Socrates believed that if people could correctly

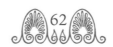

define morality and immorality, then they would almost always act according to what was right. But how can one arrive at an absolute definition of right and wrong, one that doesn't change regardless of the specific circumstances? Socrates' dialogues at the agora attempted to tackle this problem of moral complexity and relativity.

In Socrates' quest to understand and define difficult and debatable concepts, such as truth, knowledge, and right and wrong, he formed friendships, created a following, irritated strangers, and made many enemies throughout Athens. Socrates' fatal mistake was that he would question passersby without regard to their sensitivities or position in society. Some of the victims of his verbal assaults were powerful officials who did not want to lose face to a man they took to be the town's raving eccentric. Some Athenian leaders and parents of his young followers disliked Socrates' irritating nature so much that when Athens's golden age began to darken, they turned their anger against a convenient target—the old, barefooted gadfly of Athens.

FROM TEACHER TO SCAPEGOAT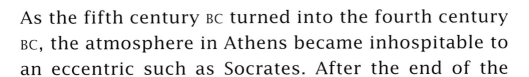

As the fifth century BC turned into the fourth century BC, the atmosphere in Athens became inhospitable to an eccentric such as Socrates. After the end of the

School of Athens (above) was painted by the Italian artist Raphael in the sixteenth century. The painting depicts ancient Greece's leading philosophers and scientists debating how to reconcile classical pre-Christian notions of philosophy with Christian beliefs. Socrates, wearing a green robe, can be seen gesturing with his hands to list the points he is making.

golden age, the previously tolerant citizens of Athens, who had once accepted Socrates and perhaps even encouraged his confrontational philosophical passion, turned suspicious and restrictive. Athenians were saddened by the death of their great leader Pericles, were worn out from years of war and plague, and were anxious about their city's uncertain future. Athens was existing in an atmosphere of instability, and Athenian society was nothing like the progressive, forward-looking one it had been only a few years before. Athenian leaders, rather than looking to the future for ways to improve their city, turned their attention instead to the past to find someone or something to blame for their recent misfortunes.

Socrates, the highly public annoyance, became a target of Athenian anger and scapegoating.

He was a well-known figure around Athens but not necessarily a well-liked one. In many ways, he was a quintessential product of the golden age that had recently ended in disgrace and defeat. Despite the fact that Athenians had lost control of their city and seen a huge portion of their population sicken and die with an unexplainable disease, Socrates carried on as he always had. He remained the calm, cool, single-minded philosopher who agitated Athenians by roping them into conversations about public morality and private matters of the soul.

This man, who was famous for his loud and public criticisms, remained uncharacteristically silent about the huge changes that were sweeping over Athens. To his enemies, the philosophical probing that Socrates had been carrying on for several decades—which was often undeniably critical, contrary, and antidemocratic—was now seen as disrespectful, unpatriotic, and increasingly intolerable.

Socrates' political views had always been out of step with the mainstream thought of Athens. As the preeminent thinker during Athens's golden age, Socrates used his prominence to voice his doubts freely about the Athenians' beloved democracy. He questioned the wisdom of having a government in which a common person could become the nation's ruler, and a state in which the ruled could also serve as the rulers. He also questioned the wisdom of people making important state decisions while being subject to the whims of a restless voting public. Instead, Socrates said that major governmental decisions should be made by "the one who knows," implying that he thought a single ruler, such as a king, should wield the power of government. He is quoted in *Memorabilia* as saying, "The one who knows should rule, and the others obey." This kind of system was similar to the government of the Thirty Tyrants, which the Spartans imposed upon Athens after the Peloponnesian War.

Socrates' political opinions may have been dismissed by Athens's leaders during the golden age, when democratic government appeared to be indestructible. In an Athens shaken by disease, defeat, and civil war, however, his views suddenly were met with less tolerance. Soon enough, an obscure poet emerged to take careful aim at Socrates in an effort to destroy the man whose unconventional—and now perhaps dangerous—ideas still attracted a large and enthusiastic following.

5 | THE TRIAL OF SOCRATES

Two Athenian politicians named Anytus and Lycon had a bone to pick with Socrates and his school of followers. Anytus, who had been a popular politician during the golden age, was stripped of power when Sparta imposed its rule of the Thirty Tyrants over Athens following the Peloponnesian War. He was greatly angered by this humiliating comedown. Athens's government had returned to the hands of its former democratic leaders by the turn of the century, after the Tyrants' leader, Critias, was killed in battle. However, many Athenian politicians were embittered by the experience and sought retaliation. However, there was no one against whom they could direct their anger, as most of the Thirty Tyrants and their Athenian allies had either fled the city or had died in battle.

Anytus, the mastermind behind the accusations, was determined to get vengeance, and he scrutinized the men of Athens to find a worthy target for his anger. His eyes landed on the rude, irreverent, antidemocratic critic holding forth at the agora, Socrates.

Anytus enlisted a poet friend, Meletus, to do his dirty work for him. Calling in a favor owed to him, Anytus urged Meletus to file charges against Socrates with the Athenian courts. Anytus did not want to file charges himself, fearing that he would fall out of favor among Athens's voters if he lost the case. Meletus was unknown to most Athenians, so he had nothing to lose. In 399 BC, Meletus brought two charges against Socrates. The first accused him of "corrupting" the youth of Athens. The second charged the philosopher with "not worshipping the gods worshipped by the state." This second charge may have been inspired by Socrates' supposed belief that he was guided by a personal divine spirit. Both crimes were punishable by death.

UNFORTUNATE FRIENDSHIPS

In his days spent walking around Athens, Socrates engaged in dialogues with many different people

and formed friendships with men from all walks of life. The company a person kept was not at issue during the open-minded golden age, but it did become a matter of scrutiny during the more fearful and repressive era that followed the defeat to Sparta at the beginning of the fourth century. A few decades earlier, Socrates had befriended three men whose friendships would come to haunt him at the turn of the century. Two of these men were soldiers who would go down in history as being primarily responsible for bringing Athens's golden age to an end.

One of these destructive friendships was formed when Socrates was serving in the Athenian army during a war with the city-state Potidaea in 432 BC. During a battle, Socrates saved the life of his fellow soldier Alcibiades. Out of gratitude and respect, Alcibiades became a loyal follower of Socrates'. He was often seen following the old sage around the agora, drawing the attention of Socrates' enemies. This ardent disciple of Socrates' is known today as the Benedict Arnold of Greece, named after the famous defector from the Continental army during the American Revolution (1775–1783) whose name became synonymous with "traitor."

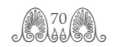

Master and pupil appear together in this circa 1780 Italian pastel-on-paper drawing entitled *Alcibiades Reprimanded by Socrates*. It is unclear why Alcibiades is being scolded by the philosopher (*seated*), but it is generally believed that the young soldier was unable to copy Socrates' spirit of self-denial and rigorous thought, even though he admired it greatly. Alcibiades developed a reputation for luxury, excessive partying, and lustful behavior, all of which must have offended the sober and morally high-minded Socrates.

Alcibiades was once a popular liberal politician in Athens's Assembly, but during the Peloponnesian War, Alcibiades secretly switched his allegiance to Sparta. In 415 BC, he took advantage of his power in the Assembly and the trust Athenians had placed in him by proposing a plan to invade the rich and powerful city-state Syracuse. He argued that the invasion would increase Athens's resources in the war against Sparta. In 413 BC, however, before the Athenians reached Syracuse, Alcibiades and the well-prepared and informed Spartan troops ambushed the surprised Athenians, killing tens of thousands of them.

Following the restoration of the Athenian government, Socrates suffered for his association with Alcibiades. To make matters worse for him, before the Peloponnesian War, Alcibiades had been accused of defacing (damaging) religious statues. Socrates had nothing to do with either Alcibiades' treason or his vandalism, and would surely have condemned both. In the courtroom, however, Meletus reminded the jurors of Socrates' ties to this sacrilegious traitor of Athens, hinting that Socrates was guilty by association. He even implied that Socrates may have been the one to urge Alcibiades to turn against his own country during the Peloponnesian War.

Another of Socrates' unfortunate acquaintances was with a former disciple named Critias. Like Alcibiades, Critias would go down in history as a traitor to Athens during the Peloponnesian War and during his time served as a major leader in the pro-Spartan Thirty Tyrants government. Unlike Alcibiades, Critias died in the battle in which the Thirty Tyrants lost control of Athens and couldn't be punished for his treachery.

Xenophon was the third man whose friendship compromised Socrates' standing in society. He was an Athenian, who became notorious for his lack of loyalty. He came from a wealthy family and was a member of the cavalry near the end of the Peloponnesian War. Like other members of this elite service, he probably sided with the Thirty Tyrants during the civil war. In 401 BC, he joined an expedition of Greek mercenaries (soldiers for hire), who were hired to help Cyrus the Younger seize the Persian crown from his brother. Socrates urged him not to go, since Cyrus was perceived as a friend of the Spartans and an enemy of Athens. Xenophon ignored his advice and went anyway. His disloyal action thus seemed to confirm the corrupting effects of Socrates' teaching on the young and probably helped convict his teacher when he faced charges in 399 BC.

THE FEAR BEHIND THE CHARGES

Anytus used these skeletons in Socrates' closet to bolster the case against him, but what really inspired Anytus's accusations was his concern for the future of Athens. What Anytus really meant by his accusations was that Socrates was corrupting the young politically, rather than morally (though he did object to Socrates' quoting somewhat lewd, or off-color, passages from Homer and Hesiod). In Anytus's eyes, the widespread adoption of Socrates' views among Athenian youth represented a grave threat to the city-state's future. Socrates himself was not a threat to Athens's democracy, as he was seventy-one years old and penniless at the time these accusations were being made, but his ideas were.

Anytus was concerned that Socrates was broadcasting his antidemocratic views to Athens's upper class youth with his criticisms of Athenian institutions and popular elections. He also felt that Socrates urged his pupils to disobey their parents (and perhaps, by extension, Athenian rulers as well) and accept his authority instead. Anytus feared that these young Athenians would embrace and spread their master's views long after Socrates' death. This was the real motivation behind his attempts to silence the

Europe's oldest surviving law code appears above. The Gortyn Law Code, from about 450 BC, was discovered on the Greek island of Crete in the nineteenth century. The code was inscribed on the wall of the town's odeon, a small theater. The inscription provides insight into the laws of the ancient Greek world, the same legal system that would decide Socrates' fate.

Athenian Courts

During the time of Socrates' trial, any citizen in Athens could file charges against another person for any kind of wrongdoing. There were no lawyers or prosecutors. Instead, the plaintiff (the person bringing the charges) and defendant each argued his or her own case. Juries were made up of male citizens who were chosen from a pool of candidates. Unlike the American jury system today, in which the jury usually unanimously decides the verdict, the jurors in an Athenian court each cast his own vote, with the majority vote deciding the defendant's fate. Juries were usually made up of a few hundred or more people to minimize the chances of a large number of jurists being bribed by either the plaintiff or the defendant.

philosopher permanently before he could win over and influence any more young minds.

SOCRATES' DEFENSE

A record of Socrates' trial appears in Plato's *Apology*, which was written long after the proceedings. According to Plato's account, in the spring of 399 BC, during which the trial was held, Socrates was at the height of his persuasive powers.

Two fourth-century-BC artifacts relating to Athenian jury procedures and trial law appear above. At top is a juror identity card, which lists the juror's name, his father's name, and the name of his neighborhood or area of residence. This identity card was used in Athens's court of justice and was discovered in the agora. The artifact below it is a bronze disc used by judges when taking a vote among jurors in order to determine a verdict. The hollow handle at the disc's center indicates the verdict was guilty. It is inscribed with the words "official voting disc." This artifact was discovered beneath the justice building in Athens's agora.

Realizing that the trial might be one of his last opportunities to address a large audience, the eloquent and verbose (wordy and talkative) Socrates took full advantage of the occasion.

Socrates used his trial not only as an opportunity to defend himself against Meletus's charges but also as a platform for the spread of his philosophy. In order to launch an effective defense of his moral character and make a mockery of Meletus and his accusations, Socrates began his testimony with a show of humility, apologizing for the likelihood that his testimony will sound familiar to his listeners. He also emphasized his innocence by mentioning his lack of familiarity with trial proceedings.

> I must beg of you to grant me one favor, which is this—If you hear me using the same words in my defence which I have been in the habit of using, and which most of you may have heard in the agora . . . or anywhere else, I would ask you not to be surprised at this, and not to interrupt me. For I am more than seventy years of age, and this is the first time that I have ever appeared in a court of law . . . Think only of the justice of my cause, and give heed to

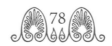

that: let the judge decide justly and the speaker speak truly (as quoted in *The Republic and Other Works*).

Socrates turned the courtroom into a forum for humiliating his accuser by showing the baselessness of Meletus's accusations and the foolishness of his character. In effect, he turned the tables on Meletus and threw his accuser on the defensive.

> He says that I am a doer of evil, who corrupt the youth; but I say, O men of Athens, that Meletus is a doer of evil, and the evil is that he makes a joke of a serious matter, and is too ready at bringing other men to trial from a pretended zeal and interest about matters in which he really never had the smallest interest (as quoted in *The Republic and Other Works*).

To rebut, or contradict, the claims that he was spreading corruption among Athens's youth, Socrates employed his famous Socratic method. He began by asking Meletus whether good people do their neighbors good, and if so, whether bad people spread evil to their neighbors. Meletus believed both

propositions were true. Then the philosopher asked Meletus if he believed that Socrates' corruption of youth was intentional. Meletus believed that it was.

Now Socrates had Meletus exactly where he wanted him. The philosopher used his accuser's replies to prove his own point. He said that if he were truly successful in the corruption of youth, then the youth would have become bad. He would have become aware of this because, as a neighbor to youths, he would be harmed by their evil, since Meletus agrees that bad people spread evil. However, Socrates claimed that he was not aware of having been harmed by any of his young neighbors. Socrates then drew the conclusion that either he did not corrupt anybody or he did so unintentionally. In either scenario, Socrates would be cleared of what he was being accused of—that he corrupted youth and did so intentionally.

Socrates discredited the second accusation brought against him regarding his worship practices by revealing Meletus's ignorance in the matter. The charge claimed that Socrates worshipped gods that were not deemed acceptable by the state. Socrates trapped Meletus into calling him an atheist, or a person who doesn't believe in any god. If Socrates was an atheist, as Meletus claimed, then Socrates did not

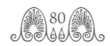

worship any gods, including those to which Athens objected. Therefore, Socrates was not guilty of the claim that he worshipped gods deemed unacceptable to Athens.

Throughout his trial, Socrates' arguments were well thought out, aggressive, and sharply focused, but he also adopted a tone of joviality as he effortlessly contradicted each of the accusations he faced and made Meletus appear more and more foolish while doing so. But as he reached the conclusion of his testimony, Socrates' tone turned serious. He shifted his attention away from insulting Meletus to talking about matters

Though often preoccupied with the ethics of daily life, Socrates was a spiritual man who believed in the afterlife. In Greek thought, the river Styx was the border between the worlds of the living and the dead. In this sixteenth-century painting by Joachim Patenier, the ferryman Charon can be seen ferrying a dead soul across the Styx to Hades, or the underworld.

of the soul with his captive audience. He urged his fellow citizens to make the improvement of their souls a priority above all others. "I do nothing but go about persuading you all, old and young alike, not to take thought for your persons or your properties, but first and chiefly to care about the greatest improvement of the soul" (as quoted in *The Republic and Other Works*).

Socrates' final words to the jury were his most contemplative and glum, as if he had a premonition of his fate. "The hour of departure has arrived, and we go our ways— I to die, and you to live. Which is better God only knows" (as quoted in *The Republic and Other Works*). Though the verdict had not yet been given, Socrates' pessimism proved justified. Out of 500 jurors, 280 found Socrates guilty as charged. He was sentenced to die.

6 | THE EXECUTION OF SOCRATES

Socrates accepted the judgment and awaited his fate calmly and patiently. Indeed, he declined two opportunities to avoid death. In an Athenian trial, the convicted was given an opportunity to propose a smaller, more lenient punishment to that urged by the accuser. Rather than doing so, however, Socrates brashly proposed not a lesser penalty that would spare his life—which many historians believe would have been accepted by the jury—but a reward for the good he had done for Athens through-out his life, both as a soldier and a public ethicist. Knowing that such an outlandish proposal would never be accepted by the jurists, Socrates asked to be supported by the state for the rest of his life and given free meals and a place to live in the Prytaneum. The Prytaneum was a sort of town hall that was a center of Athenian government and that housed the sacred fire, an eternal flame that represented the community's unity and vitality.

Eventually, Socrates did agree to offer a fine for his offenses, but the jurists were offended by his sarcastic attitude and indifference to the opportunity to spare his own life. The death sentence remained in place. Socrates remained serene, stating that he was satisfied both with his own behavior and with the jury's decision. He said he looked forward to discovering whether death was eternal sleep or a new existence in Hades (an underworld populated by the dead). If there was an afterlife, he was excited for the opportunity to quiz the heroic and wise men of antiquity who had lived and died before him. No matter what lay ahead after his execution, Socrates believed death would be a greater good than earthly life.

DOING THE RIGHT THING

Socrates' second chance to avoid death came about when his friend and pupil Crito urgently came into Socrates' prison cell at the break of dawn on the day he was to die, about thirty days after the end of the trial. He told his mentor of a plan that he and a few other friends had arranged: they had pooled their

Socrates seemed peacefully resigned to his fate and even cheerful in the days leading up to his execution. Some sense of his acceptance of the judgment against him is conveyed in this early nineteenth-century painting entitled *The Death of Socrates* by Italian artist Giuseppe Diotti. While Socrates seems at ease and calm, his followers surrounding him are openly grieving, distraught, and imploring.

money and were planning to use it to bribe prison guards to allow their friend to sneak out and flee Athens. Socrates, with his characteristic stubbornness, objected.

Socrates argued that he had made an implied contract with Athens by choosing to live in the city-state his whole life. Consequently, he felt he must abide by its laws and the decisions of its people, regardless of whether he found them to be just. He argued that it

would be wrong to escape his death sentence by conveniently breaking this contract with Athens when its laws didn't serve his personal interests.

When Crito argued that thoughts of his children's future should compel Socrates to escape, the old philosopher voiced his faith that his friends would take care of them. He said that whether he went into exile or was executed, he would not be present to raise his sons. Crito, though saddened by the idea of losing his teacher, knew that Socrates was too stubborn to be persuaded. Socrates' further words confirmed this assumption.

> Think not of life and children first, and of justice afterwards, but of justice first, that you may be justified before the princes of the world below. For neither will you nor any that belong to you be happier or holier or juster in this life, or happier in another, if you do as Crito bids. Now you depart in innocence, a sufferer and not a doer of evil; a victim, not of the laws, but of men. But if you go forth, returning evil for evil, and injury for injury, breaking the covenants and agreements which you have made with us, and wronging those whom

you ought least to wrong . . . we shall be angry with you while you live (as quoted in *The Republic and Other Works*).

Socrates was determined to do what was right, even if that meant accepting an unjust conviction without complaint and submitting to a death sentence that was undeserved. To attempt to evade or escape Athenian law, no matter how badly applied, would be like attacking the city-state and each of its citizens.

SOCRATES' LAST DAYS

Socrates did not seem afraid of death. In his last days on earth, he continued to carry on as he always had, with his thoughts focused on questions of morality. He was constantly surrounded by crowds of people who would visit him at the prison. He did not seem frightened, anxious, bitter, or angry. Socrates appeared as he always had: contemplative, calm, and eager for conversation. On the morning that Socrates was to die, he seemed to be in good spirits. He even made a joke with Crito about his chatty tendencies hours before he was to drink the deadly hemlock (a poison derived from the hemlock plant, which is in the carrot and parsnip family). Crito reported to Socrates:

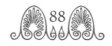

"The attendant who is to give you the poison has been telling me that you are not to talk much, and he wants me to let you know this; for that by talking, heat is increased, and this interferes with the action of the poison; those who excite themselves are sometimes obliged to drink the poison two or three times."

"Then," said Socrates, "let him mind his business and be prepared to give the poison two or three times" (as quoted in *The Republic and Other Works*).

Socrates' engagement in philosophical discussions right up to the time of his death, and his calmness before he was to drink the cup of poison, underscore the sincerity of Socrates' lifelong pursuit of truth and his faith in the supreme importance of morality.

The difficulty, my friends, is not to avoid death, but to avoid immorality; for that runs faster than death. I am old and move slowly, and the slower runner (that is, death) has overtaken me, while my accusers are keen and quick, and immorality, an even faster runner, has overtaken them (as

This 1787 painting entitled *The Death of Socrates* by French artist Jacques-Louis David shows Socrates defiantly making one final point as he reaches for the bowl of hemlock that will kill him. Socrates expressed no fear of death. Instead, whether death would turn out to be eternal sleep or the beginning of a new journey, he believed it could only be a blessing.

quoted in Don Nardo's *The Trial of Socrates*).

Convinced that he had done right and would continue to do so by submitting to Athenian law, Socrates had no fear of death. His critics, however, were immoral, according to Socrates. Therefore, they might not be so lucky in the afterlife.

THE EXECUTION

Socrates was surrounded by many of his friends in the prison cell on the day he was to die. His wife, Xanthippe, was also there with their infant son, but Socrates ordered her to leave before he drank the poison so he wouldn't have to hear her cries.

The mood in the prison cell was somber and contemplative. The philosopher's friends first talked about Aesop's fables. Then

Pl. 101.

Ethuse fétide.

This engraving depicts the leaves of a hemlock plant. Hemlock is an herb related to the parsnip family that can grow 3 to 8 feet tall (0.9 to 2.4 meters) and has a purple-spotted stem and triangular leaves. Nowadays, hemlock is usually found along roadsides and on the edge of farm fields, railroad tracks, and river banks. The entire plant is poisonous, especially its leaves and seeds. Symptoms of hemlock poisoning can range from the mild—nervousness and trembling—to the far more severe—depression, coma, and death.

Socrates asked Crito to help him pay a debt of a rooster that he owed to a healer. Later, as the time appointed for Socrates to drink the poison approached, Socrates shared his philosophies on the soul and its eternal nature with his good friends who were in the cell with him.

> And is it likely that the soul will be blown away and destroyed immediately after leaving the body? That can never happen . . . I say that the soul, itself invisible, departs for the invisible world—to the divine and immortal and rational realm, released from the error and folly of men, their fears and wild passions and all the other human ills, and dwells forever in the company of gods (as quoted in *The Trial of Socrates*).

Before Socrates was served the hemlock, he asked a prison worker what he should do after consuming the poison. Socrates was told that he should walk around his cell until he felt a numbness in his legs, at which time he should lie down and close his eyes.

Socrates did exactly as the jailer advised. Soon after lying down, Socrates passed away. He gave every indication of having died peacefully. The state of Athens had successfully condemned, silenced, and killed its gadfly.

CONCLUSION

There is little doubt that Socrates' death was unjust. In many ways, Socrates was a man truly dedicated to his country, despite his antidemocratic ideas. Though Socrates didn't support Athens's democratic government, when the city demanded his services in the army, he fought bravely for it. And when Athens condemned him to die, he obediently accepted the punishment without feeling any bitterness. When he had the chance to evade his death sentence, he refused on the grounds that he must remain loyal to the alliance he had made with his city-state, even if that meant submitting to an unjust punishment.

If Socrates was guilty of anything, it was being an annoying intellectual and bullying moralist with an abrasive personality, eccentric mannerisms, and antidemocratic views. Later generations of Greeks and members of other Western cultures saw Socrates' condemnation, conviction, and execution as a tragic breach of justice and a shameful failure of democracy. But in Athens, Socrates' death caused no great outcry and no immediate changes to society. Life carried on as usual. Anytus, the primary politician behind the charges against Socrates, rose even further in popularity and power.

Socrates was seen as someone who wanted to shake up Athenian tradition. As a result, he became associated with the waves of change—most of them distressing, destructive, and disastrous—that had swamped Athens since the end of Pericles' reign. To help Athens return to its former glory, this agent of change had to be destroyed.

It was not until years later that Socrates' execution was able to serve some greater good. Socrates' most famous pupil, Plato, was very troubled by his mentor's state-sanctioned death. The injustice served to Socrates spurred Plato to ponder morals and political justice. He studied this topic for many years throughout Greece, Italy, and Egypt before he returned to Athens to establish the Academy, a school that is regarded as the first true modern university. The Academy hosted many political and philosophical discussions over the years that would influence government and law long after the deaths of Socrates and Plato.

Perhaps what is most ironic about Socrates' ending is that it greatly benefited his reputation and his legacy, and destroyed those of his critics. If Socrates

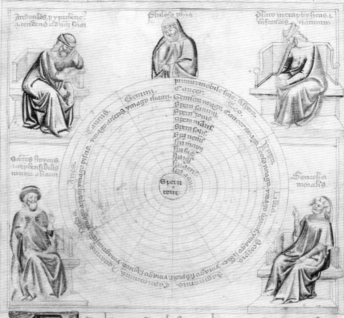

Four leading figures of classical learning appear in this fourteenth-century-AD illuminated (brightly colored and illustrated) manuscript page from the *Panegyric of Bruzio Visconti*. The three most important Greek philosophers—Aristotle, Plato, and Socrates—are joined by the Roman playwright Seneca around the page's four corners. Medieval Europe, though plunged into a period of violence and relative ignorance during the barbarian invasions, had enormous respect for these almost legendary figures of classical knowledge.

had not been killed for his unconventional ideas, he probably would have become an insignificant, perhaps even forgotten, figure in Greek philosophy. His dialogues relied on impromptu (or improvised) questions and answers. Because they weren't written down at the time, the dialogues endured only as long as the debates themselves. Socrates kept no journal or written account of his ideas. Most likely, his arguments would have disappeared soon after his death had Xenophon and Plato not had reason to preserve the memory of their mentor.

Socrates' greatest achievement is his Socratic method of questioning. Even that, however, was less a gift of a philosophic method of inquiry and more an expression of his relentless, probing personality. In the end, it was Athens that fostered the gadfly's eccentricities and his philosophical ideas, and then punished him for them. Paradoxically, it was also Athens's execution of Socrates that helped preserve his memory and enshrine his passionate commitment to knowledge, truth, and ethics—and to always searching for the knowledge of what is right.

TIMELINE

499 BC	The Persian Empire attacks Greek city-states, and Athens sends troops to aid its Greek neighbors. The Persian Wars begin.
486 BC	The Persian army destroys the Athenian Acropolis during its campaign to invade Athens.
479 BC	Persian Wars end with Persia's defeat. Athens is the leading victor and rises to prominence.
circa 479 BC	Athens forms the Delian League, a jointly funded military alliance, with other city-states as a protection against future Persian attacks.
circa 470 BC	Socrates is born on Mount Lycabettus, located on the outskirts of Athens.
460 BC	Pericles becomes statesman-general and rises quickly in Athens's Assembly. This period marks the beginning of Athens's golden age, a time of relative peace, prosperity, creativity, and reconstruction.
447 BC	Phidias directs the building of the Parthenon, a project that showcases Athens's wealth and power. The monument serves as a tribute to Athens's

patron goddess Athena, the goddess of wisdom and war.

circa 440 BC	Socrates visits the Oracle at Delphi, where he is proclaimed the wisest man of all. The oracle's declaration launches Socrates' search to define wisdom, a quest that lasts throughout his life.
432 BC	Socrates serves as a hoplite in a battle against Potidaea, a Spartan ally, during which he forms a friendship with Alcibiades, who will later betray Athens and compromise Socrates' standing in Athenian society.
431 BC	Peloponnesian War begins with Sparta and its allies pitted against Athens.
circa 431 BC	An unknown plague infects Athens, claiming at least 25 percent of Athens's population. Pericles and his family die from the plague in 429 BC.
circa 428 BC	Plato, Socrates' most famous disciple, is born.
circa 420 BC	Socrates marries Xanthippe. They eventually have three sons together.

(continued on following page)

(continued from previous page)

404 BC   The Peloponnesian War ends in Athens's defeat,
          and Sparta replaces Athens's democratic government
          with the rule of the Thirty Tyrants. This marks the
          end of Athens's golden age.

399 BC   Meletus files charges against Socrates, accusing him
          of corrupting the youth and worshipping gods not
          sanctioned by the state. Socrates goes to trial, is
          found guilty, and is sentenced to die. Socrates drinks
          a cup of poisonous hemlock and dies in prison.

GLOSSARY

Academy The school founded by Plato in 387 BC, which is regarded as the world's first true university. The institution focused on instruction of philosophy and science and was shut down in AD 529, more than 900 years after its establishment. Plato, one of Socrates' students, was partly inspired to open the school by his mentor's unjust death.

agora Marketplace. The agora served as the center of commerce and trade and as a meeting place for Athenians in ancient times. Socrates chose to engage in philosophical debates at the agora because it was the busiest spot in Athens, where his ideas would reach the greatest number of people.

Delian League A military alliance founded around 479 BC by Athens and hundreds of other Greek city-states for protection against future attacks from outsiders, especially Persians.

gadfly A person who provokes and annoys persistently. Socrates called himself the gadfly of Athens because of his constant badgering of passersby to engage them in philosophical debates.

golden age   A time of peace, prosperity, and happiness. Athens's golden age was from around 460 BC to the end of the fifth century BC. During this era, Athens was ruled by a popular democracy, the city-state had ample funds to spend on projects to improve and beautify the city, and Athenians lived in relative peace and happiness. The period is regarded as one of the most progressive times in both Athenian and Greek history.

hoplite   A Greek foot soldier who provided his own armor. During the fifth century BC, hoplites were usually drawn from the middle classes because they could afford their own military gear.

Oracle at Delphi   A shrine that was built in 1400 BC dedicated to Apollo, the god of music and the arts in the Greek city of Delphi. In ancient times, Greeks believed that a prophet was present at the shrine, and Greeks would travel to Delphi to ask the oracle for answers to any questions they had.

philosophy   Literally meaning "love of wisdom" in Greek, philosophy is a discipline that centers around the inquiry into truth and morality and the creation of a system of ideas based on the results of such inquiries.

polis   The Greek term for a city-state. In ancient Greece, there were more than 100 poleis in the

Mediterranean, each with its own separate government that was independent from the governments of other city-states.

scapegoat   A person who is forced to bear the blame for other people's sins or crimes, or for the wrongs of all of society.

Socratic method   A method of philosophical inquiry devised by Socrates that uses a series of questions to expose the weaknesses of one's assumptions and replace them with beliefs that seem closer to the truth. Socrates would pose questions such as "What is truth?" and "What is virtue?" and ask question after question until his listeners could provide a reasonable, workable definition or answer. A major characteristic of the Socratic method is that it involves conversation and debate with at least one other person.

Sophists   Sophists were highly regarded teachers in ancient Greece who traveled throughout the city-states and taught philosophy and rhetoric to their disciples for a fee.

FOR MORE INFORMATION

The Ancient Philosophy Society
Colby College
4554 Mayflower Hill
Waterville, ME 04901
(207) 872-3140
e-mail: jpgordon@colby.edu
Web site: http://www.trincoll.edu/orgs/aps

Kids Philosophy Slam
P.O. Box 406
Lanesboro, MN 55949
e-mail: info@philosophyslam.org
Web site: http://www.philosophyslam.org

Northwest Center for Philosophy for Children
P.O. Box 353350
Department of Philosophy
University of Washington
Seattle, WA 98195
e-mail: info@philosophyforchildren.org
Web site: http://depts.washington.edu/nwcenter

Society for Ancient Greek Philosophy
Binghamton University
P.O. Box 6000
Binghamton, NY 13902
(607) 777-2886 or (607) 777-2646

Society for Philosophical Inquiry
P.O. Box 3718
Williamsburg, VA 23187
Web site: http://www.philosopher.org

WEB SITES

Due to the changing nature of Internet links, the
Rosen Publishing Group, Inc., has developed an
online list of Web sites related to the subject of
this book. This site is updated regularly. Please
use this link to access the list:

http://www.rosenlinks.com/lgp/socr

FOR FURTHER READING

Aird, Hamish. *Pericles: The Rise and Fall of Athenian Democracy.* New York, NY: The Rosen Publishing Group, 2004.

Nardo, Don. *Leaders of Ancient Greece.* San Diego, CA: Lucent Books, 1999.

Powell, Anton. *Ancient Greece.* New York, NY: Facts on File, 1989.

Strathern, Paul. *Socrates in 90 Minutes.* Chicago, IL: Ivan R. Dee, 1997.

Zannos, Susan. *The Life and Times of Socrates.* Hockessin, DE: Mitchell Lane Publishers, 2005.

BIBLIOGRAPHY

Britannica Online. "Socrates." Retrieved March 2005 (http://search.eb.com/ebi/article?tocld =92771208query=socrates&ct=).

Hooker, Richard. "Greek Philosophy: Socrates." 1996. Retrieved April 2005 (http://www.wsu.edu/~dee/ GREECE/SOCRATES.HTM).

Magee, Bryan. *The Story of Philosophy.* New York, NY: DK Publishing, Inc., 1998.

Nardo, Don. *The Trial of Socrates.* San Diego, CA: Lucent Books, Inc., 1997.

Plato. *The Republic and Other Works.* New York, NY: Doubleday, 1989.

"Socrates: A Biography of Socrates' Life." LoveToKnow Corp. 2002. Retrieved April 2005 (http://www. 2020site.org/socrates).

Stone, I. F. *The Trial of Socrates.* New York, NY: Doubleday, 1980.

Turner, William. "Socrates." The Catholic Encyclopedia Online. 2003. Retrieved April 2005 (http://www. newadvent.org/cathen/14119a.htm).

Vlastos, Gregory. *Socratic Studies.* Cambridge, England: Cambridge University Press, 1993.

Xenophon. *Memorabilia of Socrates.* Retrieved March 2005 (http://thriceholy.net/Texts/ Memorabilia.html).

INDEX

ABOUT THE AUTHOR

Jun Lim first learned about the Socratic method of questioning in college. In addition to the ethical practicalities of Socrates' philosophies, she has been attracted to the study of political justice ever since hearing personal accounts of life during the Cultural Revolution in China, where she was born. Jun, like Socrates, believes that individuals can make significant contributions to society only after answering self-directed questions designed to examine one's own ethical and moral beliefs, and that each person carries a personal responsibility in the effort to create an ethical world. Jun was raised in Oregon and now lives in Brooklyn, New York.

PHOTO CREDITS

Cover (inset), pp. 3 (inset), 64–65 Scala/Art Resource, NY; cover (background), pp. 3 (background), 90–91 © Francis G. Meyer/Corbis; pp. 7, 48–49 akg-images/Peter Connolly; p. 8 akg-images/Gilles Mermet; p. 12 *Peace* by Aristophanes in the Duke Papyrus Archive, Special Collections Library, Duke University; p. 12 © Bettmann/Corbis; pp. 15, 28, 31, 39, 47, 62, 81 Erich Lessing/Art Resource, NY; p. 19 Réunion des Musées Nationaux/Art Resource, NY; p. 22 Private Collection, Archives Charmet/ Bridgeman Art Library; pp. 37, 52–53 Originally published in Historical Atlas of the World, © J. W. Cappelens Forlag A/S, Oslo, 1962. Maps by Berit Lie. Used with permission of J. W. Cappelens Forlag; p. 40 Louvre, Paris, France, Lauros/Giraudon/Bridgeman Art Library; p. 42 Bildarchiv Preussischer Kulturbesitz/Art Resource, NY; p. 44 © Birmingham Museums and Art Gallery; p. 51 Private Collection, Boltin Picture Library/Bridgeman Art Library; pp. 54, 77 akg-images/John Hios; p. 59 Musée de la Ville de Paris, Musée Carnavalet, Paris, France, Archives Charmet/Bridgeman Art Library; p. 71 Private Collection, Charles Plante Fine Arts/Bridgeman Art Library; p. 75 © Kevin Schafer/Corbis; pp. 82–83 The Art Archive/Museo del Prado Madrid/Dagli Orti; p. 86 The Art Archive/Museo Civico Cremona/Dagli Orti; p. 92 Private Collection, The Stapleton Collection/Bridgeman Art Library; p. 96 Giraudon/Art Resource, NY.

Designer: Tahara Anderson
Photo Researcher: Jeffrey Wendt